Pebble Plus

Exploring the Galaxy

Earth

by Thomas K. Adamson

Consulting Editor: Gail Saunders-Smith, Ph.D.

Consultant: James Gerard
Aerospace Education Specialist, NASA
Kennedy Space Center, Florida

Capstone
press

Mankato, Minnesota

PINEWOOD MEDIA CENTER

Pebble Plus is published by Capstone Press
151 Good Counsel Drive, P.O. Box 669, Mankato, Minnesota 56002
http://www.capstone-press.com

1 2 3 4 5 6 08 07 06 05 04 03

Library of Congress Cataloging-in-Publication Data
Adamson, Thomas K., 1970–
    Earth / by Thomas K. Adamson.
    p. cm.—(Pebble Plus: exploring the galaxy)
    Summary: Simple text and photographs describe planet Earth.
    Includes bibliographical references and index.
    ISBN 0-7368-2111-2 (hardcover)
    1. Earth—Juvenile literature. [1. Earth.] I. Title. II. Series.
QB631.4 .A33 2004
525—dc21   2002155599

Editorial Credits
Mari C. Schuh, editor; Kia Adams, designer; Alta Schaffer, photo researcher; Eric Kudalis, product planning editor

Photo Credits
Bruce Coleman Inc./Phil Degginger, 16–17
Corbis Images, 19
Digital Vision, 5 (Venus)
Digital Wisdom, 13
Image Source, 20–21
NASA, 1, 4 (Pluto); JPL, 5 (Jupiter); JPL/Caltech, 5 (Uranus); NSSDC, 15
PhotoDisc Inc., cover, 4 (Neptune), 5 (Mars, Mercury, Earth, Sun, Saturn), 7 (both), 8–9; PhotoDisc Imaging, 11

Note: When Earth is viewed from space, Earth's north is not always oriented "up."

Note to Parents and Teachers

The Exploring the Galaxy series supports national science standards related to earth science. This book describes and illustrates the planet Earth. The photographs support early readers in understanding the text. The repetition of words and phrases helps early readers learn new words. This book also introduces early readers to subject-specific vocabulary words, which are defined in the Glossary section. Early readers may need assistance to read some words and to use the Table of Contents, Glossary, Read More, Internet Sites, and Index/Word List sections of the book.

Word Count: 148
Early-Intervention Level: 15

Table of Contents

Earth

Earth is the only planet in the solar system where people and animals live. Earth and the other planets move around the Sun.

The Solar System

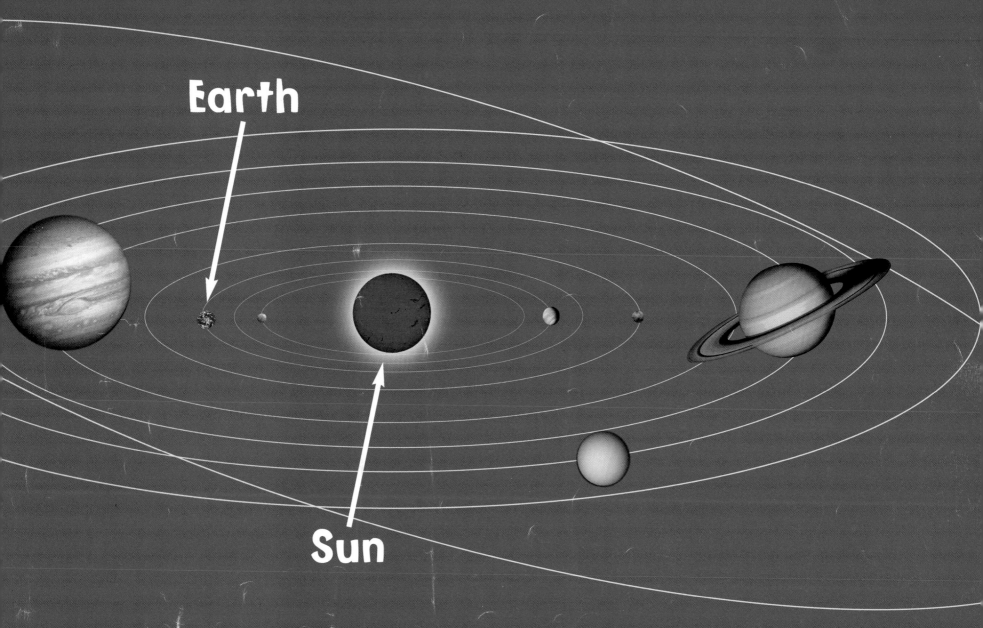

Earth

Sun

It takes about 365 days
for Earth to move around
the Sun one time. Earth
moves around the Sun
once each year.

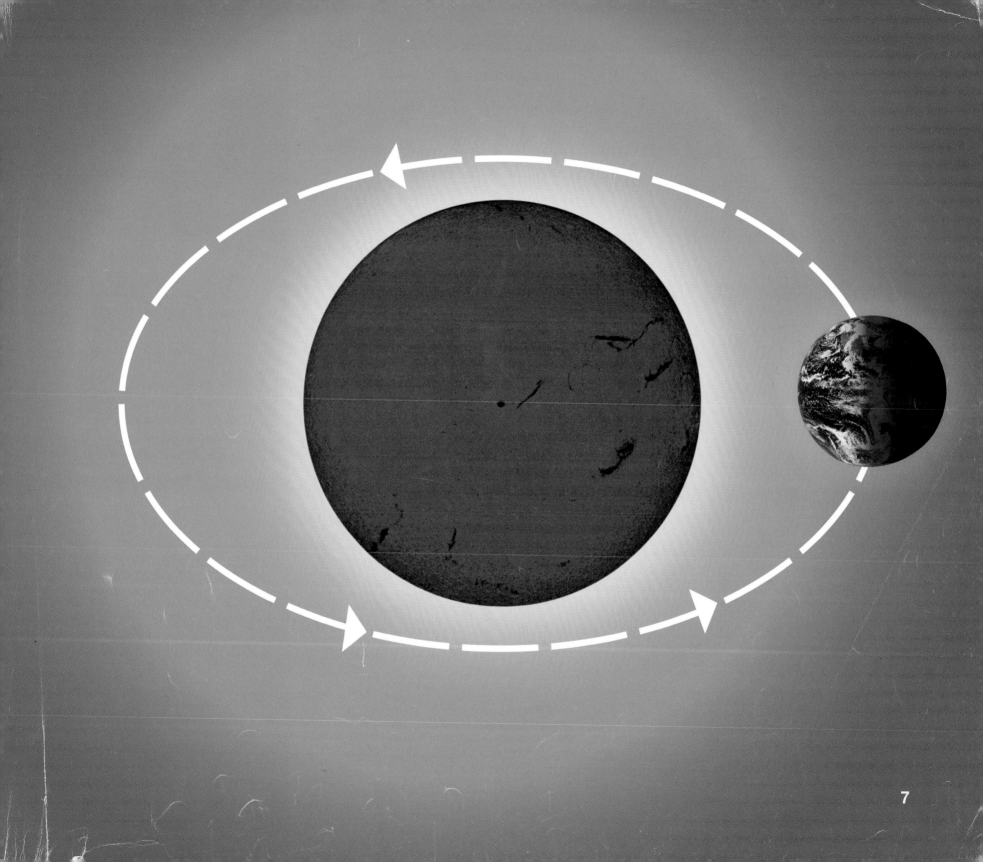

Air and Land

People and animals breathe the air on Earth. Life cannot survive without air.

9

Earth is made of rock
and metal. The center of
Earth is hot molten metal.

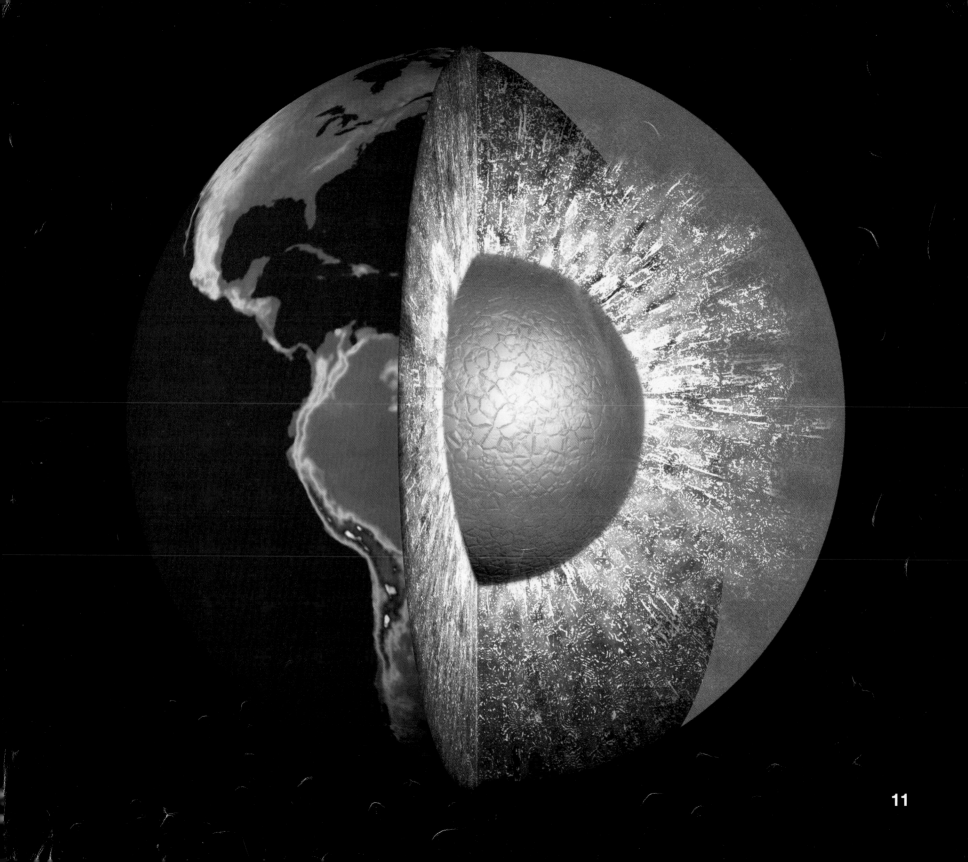

Water

Water covers most of
Earth's surface. People
and animals cannot
survive without water.

13

Most of Earth's water is in the oceans. The water makes Earth look blue from space.

Weather

Earth has many types of weather. Different places on Earth get different kinds of weather.

People and Earth

Earth has one moon.

People can easily see

the Moon from Earth.

Earth gives people and
animals all they need to live.
Earth has air, food, water,
and the right temperature.

Glossary

breathe—to take air in and out of the lungs; people and animals must breathe to live.

molten—melted by heat

moon—an object that moves around a planet; Earth has one moon.

ocean—a large body of salt water; the five oceans of Earth are the Atlantic, Pacific, Arctic, Antarctic, and Indian Oceans.

planet—a large object that moves around the Sun; Earth is the third planet from the Sun; there are nine planets in the solar system.

Sun—the star that the planets move around; the Sun provides light and heat for the planets.

weather—the conditions outside; weather can be hot or cold, wet or dry, calm or windy, or clear or cloudy.

year—the period of time in which Earth makes one trip around the Sun; one year is about 365 days.

Read More

Clark, Stuart. *Earth.* The Universe. Chicago: Heinemann Library, 2003.

Furniss, Tim. *The Earth.* Spinning through Space. Austin, Texas: Raintree Steck-Vaughn, 2001.

Kerrod, Robin. *Planet Earth.* Planet Library. Minneapolis: Lerner Publications, 2000.

Internet Sites

Do you want to find out more about Earth and the solar system? Let FactHound, our fact-finding hound dog, do the research for you.

Here's how:

1) Visit *http://www.facthound.com*

2) Type in the **Book ID** number: **0736821112**

3) Click on **FETCH IT**.

FactHound will fetch Internet sites picked by our editors just for you!

Index/Word List